INFRANGIBLE

ESSENTIAL POETS SERIES 256

Canada Council **Conseil des Arts**
for the Arts **du Canada**

ONTARIO ARTS COUNCIL
CONSEIL DES ARTS DE L'ONTARIO

an Ontario government agency
un organisme du gouvernement de l'Ontario

Canadä

Guernica Editions Inc. acknowledges the support of the Canada Council
for the Arts and the Ontario Arts Council. The Ontario Arts Council
is an agency of the Government of Ontario.

We acknowledge the financial support of the Government of Canada.

INFRANGIBLE

Carol Barbour

GUERNICA
EDITIONS
TORONTO • BUFFALO • LANCASTER (U.K.)
2018

Michael Mirolla, editor
David Moratto, cover and interior design
Carol Barbour, Cover artwork, *Head in the Hands*,
oil on wood, 20 × 27 cm., 2014.
Guernica Editions Inc.
1569 Heritage Way, Oakville, (ON), Canada L6M 2Z7
2250 Military Road, Tonawanda, N.Y. 14150-6000 U.S.A.
www.guernicaeditions.com

Distributors:
University of Toronto Press Distribution,
5201 Dufferin Street, Toronto (ON), Canada M3H 5T8
Gazelle Book Services, White Cross Mills
High Town, Lancaster LA1 4XS U.K.

First edition.
Printed in Canada.

Legal Deposit—Third Quarter
Library of Congress Catalog Card Number: 2017964542
Library and Archives Canada Cataloguing in Publication
Barbour, Carol, 1960-, author
Infrangible / Carol Barbour. -- First edition.

(Essential poets series ; 256)
Poems.
ISBN 978-1-77183-278-6 (softcover)

I. Title. II. Series: Essential poets ; 256

PS8553.A758I54 2018   C811'.54   C2018-900143-7

For my family and friends

In memory of my mother,
Elinor McKinnon Barbour (1927–2008)

Contents

The Broken Vase

Gigantomachy

The Broken Vase

At First

We were quiet,
    genuflecting in silence.

Eyes closed, then opened,
    a sleepy interchange

of fish in water, kissing
    against glass.

We beckoned to one another
    wading in the ringlets,

arriving in the mutual embrace,
    accepting

the most important person,
    of nothing.

We settled in for the night.
    Thank you.

For what?
    For giving yourself.

Did I do that?
    Yes.

But what of the glass?
    It is broken.

You Took Me In

With open arms. And cringed
when you found the pain.

We persisted in slavish devotion
to the idea of a shared humanity,

though the glue couldn't hold.
And in the end we became discouraged

by the task.
No longer speaking

about the how or the why,
we blew off course,

left the sheets on our bed tangled,
ignoring the alarm-clock chime.

Eventually we donned shields
to protect against everything.

Do you recall when I exposed
my breasts to fight your cause?

No? You found me wanting,
superfluous.

These days I live in a vase,
a terracotta urn that is safe —

enough to sit in with my back
to the sun.

Figment

The vase is painted with fine strokes
prancing about in the guise of Apollo.

I raise my pencil with an open hand,
enunciate the lines that trail obscure,

ignite fire from broken wings,
ruffle feathers across a brow.

Pad through the history of art
and land on a painting by Titian.

Danae is reverent before Jupiter
who showers gold upon her swoon.

Trading pencil for brush,
I sweep in dots, glint shadows.

A figure is the subject,
the line I continue to draw upon.

The face emerges as a figment
through the faded splatter.

With a brush, I plunge indigo
into the shell of the cheek.

A small crevice is formed
in the mixing of pink and blue.

Headless Woman

Divided from, tucked into.
A part of the whole,
yet severed from the body

that gave her life.
The headless woman floats
in a Cartesian equation.

A chorus calls out for unity,
sibilant voices ruminating
on the resurrection myth.

The dome of the Pantheon
floats, the oculus is distinct
from that which came before.

A letter flutters down,
addressed to the woman
who holds her head in her hands.

Not a saint, rather a deletion,
she makes up conversations,
paints emblems for the perplexed.

Despite the rupture, she exists
from thumb to head,
including the anus, her foot.

Connected to a convulsion,
a network of spasms, she
arrives in a gush.

Truth

i.

Non-described nudes
take the solemn vow
to stand in for abstraction.
What would it matter
if her hair were blonde, black or white?
Who would notice if she concealed
a knife beneath her garment,
within the folds of her expanding organ?

I want to touch your symbol,
stroke your essence,
even if you are a stand-in
for something else.
I'll give you back your life,
breathe oxygen into your clay lung.
Clear the mucous
from your stubborn cough.

What's it like in the well?
Can you make your own light?
The fire they stole from Zeus.
Is it warming you in the depths?

ii.

The waters have become murky,
full of strange and unusual sounds.
Fronds resemble boneless
fish swooning along the scum.

My skin is too soft to touch,
immersed as I am in
mineral springs
that are supposed to heal.

Clichés come to haunt me
in this watery safe.
Terms such as these
float in suspension, luring me
to hook one, cast it on the page.
Must I omit these pearls
that come between us?
Truth is a grain of hope.

Tones of violent imagery,
a mute voice, becoming.

iii.

Without cliché, I am nothing.
How do I make the leap into a new language?
One that has not been handed round like coins.
I know that silver means self-conscious mirror —
I dug one up in the garden.
It was scratched and dull
like the stone mirrors of Rome
though definitely 19th century —
a time I find myself within.
The flow of industrial waste ...

Truth polishes her mirror.
Dark-haired, demure,
then violently angry,
she drives a pair of scissors
into the opened book.
She's much better now.

I had to take her hand.
She was unsure of the way.

Here you will be fine.
Asylum.
Yes, she whispered.
A strand of hair caught
the corner of her mouth.
She didn't seem to notice
when I tapped down the lid.

Eversion

In the vessel
there is a place of respite,
of comfort, enchantment,
and a distant echo of loss.

A child is born of the union
between matter
and possibility.

Training her sight on a path
to freedom,
she runs uphill, takes hold
of a dangling rope.

Fortuna evades the grip
of chance,
turns away,
and manages to balance
on the revolving ball,
gyrating.

She spins and the moment
is elusive.
Practicing
to make perfect,
she falters and forgets.

Cognizant of the possibility
of another diversion,
she steadies herself.

At the Edge of the Forest, in the Long Grass

Remind me of all the things we were going to do
before and after you fluttered out the door.

I'm absent, it seems, before the scrutiny of important people —
their tyranny of paper, of need replaced with *niente*.

Sent out in a bright day, I shrink back.
A childhood depression, an adolescent crush.

Mistaken for the one who counts. No matter
the words keep coming, floating in the sky,

spelling out puffed up consolations,
brief murmurs in hushed compliance.

I pierce the balloon, hold the air
inside for as long as it takes.

Inter-verse

My body lightens
with every step that brings me closer to
and away from what was home.

Walking dulls the senses,
and I forget the bed, the couch, the life
I shared with another.

I traipse in the dust,
arrange for a transition
from what was then to something else.

I am not measured
by the things around me,
the ticket stubs, phone numbers.

These objects are without claim.
I am not the person who won the lottery
or walked around the globe in record time.

Revelling in fleshy absorptions,
I intermix the water and oil,
fill the spaces in between lines.

A residue is discernible
in the fragrance that remains.
An homage to the absence of you.

Farewell to Woodsyman

To think you drove
all this way for me and my mossy divulgence.
I'll take it.

Arched and breathless,
then beached on the cove of my neck,
you belong to me.

Like a cup with its saucer
I am sipped and it is warm and homey
to come and go again.

Woodsyman, this past year
you have not earned a penny and live in a trailer
behind your brother's house.

You encounter your ancestors
when you walk in the pine woods and give thanks
with every moccasin step.

In the city, you emerge
as Prince Mercantile, freshly pressed and ready
with yet another business plan.

Even though you improvise
five hours away, we walk on the same earth.
I'm getting used to that.

Half-Mast

Poised to replay the dream sequence
even though I dread,
the long night.

Taut with seismic vibrations,
I yield to the outcry.
It's all I can do to keep my feet on the ground.

I open the gate as you slither past
to a world of freedom.
Your hand flapping with forgiveness.

I try to keep in touch, saying I only
want to be friends,
but you are finished with us.

I dust and wonder why we parted.
The door knobs are sticky, requiring elbow grease
to clean.

I am living at half-mast,
cluttered with boxes
filled with photographs of your smile.

No Marriage No Kids

My part-time man has a twin
    who follows him out the door
    and withers up the street.

When he hits the highway
    I am etched out of his membranes.
    So far so good.

By the time he reaches home
    I am a small burst of scent.

A week goes by and he begins to stir,
    but waits.

Then a month passes and
    he can hold off no longer.

He calls to say he's coming to town.
        Are you free?

Sure, I had no plans,
    just in case.

He offers the moment, the lack-lustre past,
    the platinum future.

Holds me briefly,
        but completely.

What more can I want?
    Much more, maybe less.

The Collective

A spring-fed river flows even in winter.
A pull of watercress is yanked into a green streak.
The stream endures and in that sense
one can know how to live by dreaming.

I flow, but sometimes I run up
against the dam, the boards and the surge.
My heart quivers, the race is on.
Still I am flowing.

The watery life is moist with possibilities.
Fluctuating in the moment, shut
and then flung open. I am caught
in the expectation of release.

Pausing to glean, to dig,
to find turtle eggs in the sand.
A worn-out blanket dredged up
and wrapped around the body.

Old culture ferried across the sea,
raised in porcelain dishes, strong boxes.
Angry men with drinking problems
ignore the women who wiped their bums —

to resist the flow, to dam the past.
The grinning faces of ancestors
so shocking at times, their skeletal
smiles loom and terrify.

Mothers wear earrings
the size of burdened nightmares.
Wind, an instrument of passion
torturing the walls of the flimsy house.

Runaway.
Run till all the old-lady
tea bags are used for a third time.
Wrung out and silenced.

Husbands, children,
and their children
run. The perfected posture gone,
forever lost in the decorated tin box.

Caught up in a pattern
leading back to the collective night
where people talk in their sleep,
even though their heads are no longer.
attached at the neck.

Art History

Is about losing one's head over images.
The body in London,
the head in Copenhagen.

Vanquished, carried away
in the night through clandestine networks,
beheaded subjects make their claims

of selfhood known.
The head of the crime-unit is taking
account of lost objects.

There's no escape from becoming
a subject like Robin Williams
in the film, *Baron Munchausen*

when he raves
that his body is trapped,
estranged from his mind.

What do art historians study?
Among other things they look at ancient coins,
amulets, hoards along the Thames,

The Bronze and Iron Ages,
Roman Britain at Bath and Somerset,
piles of coins hammered

in animal bones. Tree trunks
inside jars and along riverbeds.
Art persists when currency fails.

Finding without Looking

A copy of Caravaggio's *Deposition*
in the *Chiesa Nuova*
is too dark to see.
No lamp to feed coins into a box,
no *lux* ambulatory.

Mais or *perché* I can see it from memory.
Because the original is in the Vatican
and this dim reproductive image
is disappearing from sight.
This darkness is important.
The copy is vestigial.

As I leave I notice a fresh marble
entablature, newly installed on the
adjacent wall.
It reads: Cy Twombly (1928-2011)
The modern man of weathered scrawl
has claimed the space.
Darkness has censored the *tenebrist*
yet the white marble of Twombly's tomb
glistens.

On an angle, absorbed in an epic language,
comes the round bell-sound of Twombly
from beyond the darkened blackboard
of childhood.

His circular neural system of elliptical alphabets
keeps time with the Roman
tick of antiquity.

Self-Portrait

Giovanni Paolo Lomazzo (1538-1600) —
a painter till blindness forced him to lay down his brush
at the age of thirty-three.
His work had the quality of *vagare* —
to wander,
to charm
in order to
figurate.

His theory was a Renaissance form of pantheism:
all living things animated by the same breath.
Pagan renewal,
self-fashioning in the guise and attitude of Bacchus.
The *sylvan academicians* welcomed Lomazzo into their club —
the brotherhood of the *Accademia della Val di Blenio.*

He portrayed himself dressed in the garb of a shepherd.
On his hat was pinned a golden escutcheon of a watering can,
a kind of emblem denoting the Bacchic rites of wine and song.
An ironic stance, no doubt.

A scholar, an artist, a theoretician.
Gardener, a man between worlds.
The artist is not a director,
rather a magician, conscious that the universe is governed
by natural laws which at times seem arbitrary.
Such a universe is made visible
through the figuration of one's own likeness.

I Wouldn't Say This if I Didn't Care

A wise old bird tracks
the movements of a mouse in a fallow field.
Distress can mess up a sunset.

If I take too long to answer the call
don't blame me for dawdling all the way
back home.

Because when the eagle frowns
I feel anxiety
edging in, and all I can do is hang my head.

Around him I feel insubstantial
most of the time, and I want to prove him wrong,
though I seldom get to make the point.

He has my attention again.
Equal portions of fascination and dread spin around.
Why am I so fascinated by his inscrutable manoeuvres?

He urges me to go first, out of courtesy,
and I consent, resigned to the terms of our relation,
though all the while careening out of range.

In this orchestrated space, he insists on winning
and I surmise that the only way we can coexist
is if I stand way over here,

close my ears, my eyes especially.

Last Resort Club

This is the last time
I walk this hall
or clean these dishes.

This is the last time
I drive in the country
or attend the theatre alone.

Because I now have a place to go.
I am following
a long line of devout people.

We have signed on
to live our remaining days
captivated by smiles.

I arrive when my name is called,
greet the mattress in my cell.
It is naked, though shaped with the strain
of the one who came before.

I am reminded of my mother
who carried me for as long as she could.
I think of her lying in a hospital bed,
fighting for life,

then succumbing.
I now have a place to go.
No longer walking, but carried.

Taboo

Mary Magdalene's eyes tear up
when she recalls the last-time she touched
a god.

Off she goes,
bouncing to the desert with her lustrous red curls,
clasping the alabaster urn.

Her secret is safe,
along with his silky hand,
the moistened cheek.

Titian's painting of *Mary Magdalene*
is the mirror, the conduit
to the longing.

Her eyes are bowls of water,
quivering and spilling over.
She steadies herself by grasping her heart.

Her lips open
and whisper the words:
Am I this body?

When the security guard leaves the room
I reach out to touch the painting,
stop just in time.

Chorus

If all the voices that reside inside of me
attempt to consolidate and focus on one, just one goal,
that could be interesting for a time, but also tiring.

If all the singing people that hide in the base of my throat
could sing one song in key, in harmony,
would I be able to join the chorus?

If I could hear myself above the persuasive voices
that crowd near the gate of humanity,
I might have a chance at being heard.

If I could walk and sing and talk and hear,
and also, pay attention, that could be interesting,
though probably too intense to hold for long.

The conductor may decide that the music is too complex,
the beat overpowering, the pitch too shrill to perform.
Despite the intervention, I continue to unravel the tracks,

learn to play more than one instrument at a time.
I know there are limits to fantasy.
Eventually it resolves in form and pattern.

If I could hold on to one sound from the orchestra,
I may find the link from now to eternity,
between sound and sounding.

Self-Storage

An artist in a certain apartment building keeps smiling
even though she doesn't feel well. Her life is an abridged
version of the epic she wanted to become.
Love is unattainable, recognition elusive as ever.

What she once valued is broken or dated,
languishing in a storage locker.
She needs more room, but the universe is shrinking
and there's no time to start anew, no room to make room.

In a crevice behind a washing machine in the basement
lies a sheaf of papers,
marked by shame and retractions.
Nearby, a stack of paintings and camping gear.

In the mix are dust balls and dead bugs
colonizing a child's head of hair.
A reminder of dull objects and people
pressing down on squishy private parts.

Despite this mess of human record, one image prevails:
a match and a sudden flame, all consuming, all cleansing.
It licks the trembling hand, inhales the 1960s wallpaper,
slithers along the electrical wires, combusting in a huff.

It isn't long before the fire trucks
converge, the residents take to the street.
But the artist in apartment number four refuses to leave
despite the pleas, Jump! Save yourself. We can catch you.

Instead she throws out a few pictures, some books.
Luckily her cat sails down like a barn owl, unscathed.

Now that I have your attention I'd like to read you a poem.
Get ready. If the afterlife is an empty storage locker,
then I'd rather not go ...

In that luxurious moment, she is eclipsed by a torrent of
    water.
Within seconds the main wall heaves and falls.
A multiplying rage consumes apartments 3, 2, 1, 1A.
Number four is the last to go.

Time to Move On

Returning to the same place at a different time,
a dog pees on a crooked telephone pole.
I roam about my past,
curious to see how I've changed after all this time.

I stop to take inventory. Am I okay?
Any better? Worse?
Where do I belong?
Can't be sure.

An array of circular signals,
low flying,
bombing the same place —
re-configured, though never the same.

Re-acquainted when moistened,
the barn swallow chases the cat.

What is Being at 4:00 a.m.?

A contradiction,
the need to freeze and get on with it,
to melt despite the danger—
the provision of being alone.

Core is ground down,
irregular edges worn as well.

The moment is vast.
Infinite, in the sense
of being full of want,
of hope.

A mass of confusion,
of dread and a vague recollection
that something remains undone.

The moment holds the ache
along with joy,
rocking the heart
in the cradle of being alive.

When safety slips away
at four in the morning I try
to go back to sleep, but today
I get up.

Take a shower, cry
for no apparent reason
when the water hits my flesh.
At least my body knows.

I dress even though
it's too early, fall asleep briefly,
then awaken
just in time to meet myself.

Fortune Telling Doll

Queen Victoria had one or was it Elizabeth I?
A doll with pages of platitudes,
famous quotations,

fables,
tricks for finding oneself in the words of another.
Embracing the confusion of self in focus,

out of context,
seen through the lens
of another.

Gigantomachy

Mama

When I return home from school
there is nothing left but an empty vase.
Her strawberry preserves are depleted,
reminding me of the sweetness in her eyes.

I memorialize our conversations,
reconstruct our affinity.

It is a broken trek
back to myself, knowing
she's no longer
home.

I look for her in the nest of knitting,
by the phone, the TV remote.
I no longer find her
surrounded by books
and pictures of her hummingbirds,
recalling the ones that returned
every summer.

The red nectar was always clean
and free of bugs, thanks to mom.
A couple of tiny helicopters
savage and self-centred
took all
she had to offer,
and then some.

I was one of her admirers,
and drifted away
from the centre,
waiting for a chance
to be
me
in the presence
of
she.

Grandma

Storm doors and windows
lock and sink into night.

Faces mashed against the mulch of carpets,
smoke-laden with tobacco.
A descent into shady conversations,
fall-out on synthetic carpet
that was soft once, and now abrasive.
Split ends.

Peering at the stormy seascape above the couch
where Grandma lounged, watching
the adults smoke cigarettes and drink on Sundays
amidst the waste and necessity of work.

Grandma ruled with her cane and her dog,
the yappy Chihuahua Corgi mix,
the perimeter policed by
her vigilant Siamese cat.

She found comfort in
the beauty of animals and art,
temporary relief in
a world turned upside-down,
pause in the anger
beneath the connective tissue.

Silver spoon, not in this case.
You must be toughened —
calloused so as not to feel a thing.
Child, you are too thin-skinned.
Grandma will make you hide from evil.
No one will ever find you.
No one.

Buzzer strikes.
Next round.
Doorbell rings with insistence,
recalling the Beckett play,
interminable silences,
the variety store circus.

Long hours of expectation,
of potential customers.
You could be the one
in radar range,
a familiar part of the past,
inherent.

Redrawing the room,
I am smaller than
before.
In the brainwash of hoarding,
one is never enough.
I came too late.
I am too early.
Come back later.

Garner some soup
into the pot, stir
before the water boils dry.
Cook up the food
and rest assured.
If you believe that
then you are already
too far gone.

Tall Grandma,
I revered your graceful moves,
your curves,
and the strange dirge
you used to play
on the piano.
The uplift of your hair,
a spiral knot,
shaped with pins,
and managed
with frequent handling.

I recall your silhouette,
attenuated, majestic,
and threatening to overpower.

Gigantomachy

i.

Floating on the gust of the proletariat
lifted by the petrol that flushes from
a hole in the ground,

driven by a bald-head man
who curses,
he didn't sleep last night.

I curve in the wind and
carve the air —
an aluminum blade.

A journey
that sheds a light on the past,
a flood before the future gate.

All that's needed in this moment
is the memory of a child,
who goes wandering in the woods,

her pockets flush with handfuls of wind,
ribcage opened
in order to breathe.

She flies above the clouds
and descends with accelerating
force, into the land of the Queen.

Something small,
and aberrant
is nestled upon the topography—

a rusty trailer
parked beneath the overpass,
hidden by piles of garbage.

Stateless citizens pick through the filth,
make beds from what is safe.
Left behind they organize.

As the plane descends,
wild animals scatter,
and the people by the river burrow in.

Wedged along the bank
below the elevated highway,
they garden and sort out

the communal property.
In the early morning, they rise to work
without wages in the broad daylight.

Crashing in the woods,
adjacent to the flight pattern
of a bald-head pilot

who should have known better.
Alas! The lust released
in full body, overturned dirt.

A pause in the chaotic stamping
of feet upon cobblestones,
of cups raised on patios.

An antidote of dandelion roots,
supposed to cure just about anything,
including cancer.

When there is little to eat,
anything will have to do,
though one has to wonder –

what is the most nutritious?
Why did we land here?
No worries!

It will become clear
in time, it will come about
in the dream of arrival.

This is only day one.

ii.

Now what?
The immaculate conception
has lost its meaning

though the hand
reaches in the same
way as it has always

done.
Reaching out
to touch the light.

Do not back away
from the banquet,
the vision

of the eternal supper,
of being seen,
at the table.

Take your leave
through the corridor,
slip past the crowds that gather.

Step on the marble slab,
gaze at the club-fisted
giants.

The ones who fell
from Olympus
while riding too fast on their chariots.

Bare-bum,
they ascend in the night sky.

Magnified

i.

Trapped and folded,
the laundry done.
What a load
forced through
the small peephole
that sheds light
on the former
speck of being —
the one that haunts,
the shadow
angled.

Clever hair ornament,
mouthpiece — self
aggrandizing a former life.
Chat with a neighbour
over art house films.

ii.

Snails creep
in a dark slumber
of meandering slime —
come and rescue
the poor who live
on the other side of town
where the sewage is treated
and the race track
used to be.

No matter,
I'll continue to wait
for you by the window.
Dressed up for dinner
in my very best.
Even my dentures
sparkle.
No kidding.

iii.

Ochre-coloured lichen
splattered on rocks.
Lake water clear, then mercurial.
A divine nectar exudes
a constant supply of fresh air.
A party of humans descend
upon the metamorphosis
of a May fly.

A ball is spinning
by the window, turning
soft shoulders against me
where sharp objects
are buried
in the round,
made smooth
and partial.

A move into the fray
to buy groceries
and bus tickets.
A blank schedule
in chalk, on slate.

Roll back the night,
the deluge of twits,
bites and boils
on the neck
where the scent of ear wax
compels the insects to come.
Come and taste me.

Seeds are lying on the forest floor
and scrunch like puffed rice
as feet press and seep
into the compositing earth.

iv.

Beside the fluffy mat
the stream is too cool to step in,
yet warm enough to melt the snow
piling on the ledge.

In summer comes the budding,
the torpedoes of wild roses.
How do they thrive
with no one to care for them?
I want to bring a bouquet home
and force them to drink
tap water from a vase.
How profane.

Embossed without warmth or breath,
shuffling through brambles
against pewter laden skies.
Wondering if there is something else
to what is known and what actually
happened.
To recollect
without grasping
for balance.

Drained of the furtive sadness,
alone with the spindly trees.
Hawthorn groves with sharpened points,
interwoven as crowns for ascension.

And I'm safe I guess,
to rest back
without speech,
and listen
while staring
at a blank piece of sky.

v.

Snails return from the damp
silt and I can capture them
if I want to,
place them in a jar,
though it all comes down
to the same time and place
where the old folks ache
on worn out couches
that no longer bounce back.
They stroke a sore bone, a tender point,
all the while dreaming of a place
that used to be.

Fumes can overwhelm
on the way to the variety store,
but I manage somehow to clatter
back home before the spooky ones
come out,
with their strange music
raising their lips
to an empty bottle
calling out Mama,
Mama.

Raise a glass!
Sing a tune for me, Deary,
in a key that I know.
That's it! You've got it!

vi.

Me and the dog,
the flea and the fruit fly
line up for our provisions.
Some impatient, others without hunger.
We munch on slats of wood,
salvaged from the hulls of ships.
A sail becomes a cape
slung across the back
of the variety store owner.
Tenacious with our names
like the hard candy
she used to dish out
into our grimy little hands,

open mouths ready for
the honey-sting drop.
Her jaw cracking
when she laughed
and slapped her thighs.

Looming over the counter,
her mournful eyes
magnified like tunnels.

We made our way home
for years returning,
conjoining
followed
by a clank
as the latch
slid into place.

Innocents

A gaping chasm is opening up
to admit a new crop of innocents.

The mouth of *truth* is eating
a mob of minuscule fools
that run on toothpick legs
to the sound of old songs,
the words forgotten.

Melodies imparted
in the flaps of being heard,
buried in the sludge of the canal.
We can go further,
unless we're willing to burrow in.

If all goes well the monsters will retreat
and the rock face will crumble.
The minuscule fools will land in the deep,
joined at last by their friends.

In the meantime, we mill about,
some of us with hair, others in poodle wigs.
We tug and pull at the tender parts,
complaining and yelping till sleep.

Spider War

Sensing the approach,
the cocoon absorbs the tingling,
the hoary touch of the tin amulet
stored away in the cupboard,
that is not bare.

The spider in the hand criss-crosses
the eye in the glove, an emblem
in the all believing.
Why do you look at me that way?
Why do you look like me?

I am afraid when you grip
my head in your hands,
hold fast a vision of the person
I am supposed to be.
You are too rough.
This is forced.

Push on, cello on.
Smooth over the fragmentary parts,
the fractured sop.
I have witnessed your sudden cruelty
and I don't believe
for an instant that you meant no harm.

If shifting in your seat
helps you cope with fear,
or whatever it is that eats at your bones,
then go ahead.
Smash the china.

Is it the death rattle
that causes you to raise your voice
in rage? Violence makes us all
children again.

You are so big, towering over me,
blotting out the sun and then leaving.
Abandoned at the side of the road,
impotence is poised and still.

The crutches are placed at the altar,
and thanks are given to the blind spots,
the offerings, the engulfed moments.
The bath water is tepid
and threatens to overflow.

I can see you there, lathering up your hands
pulling at the flesh that burns with fever.
If we are killing our time together
which one of us will survive?

Lake Huggers

Trolling,
blessing our journey
with an abbreviated prayer,
whistling in tune.
Herons dive and carps roll.
We merge and collapse
in a mid-day nap.

Anchor me here in sleep.
Tomorrow take me out
on the lake.
I want to see the shore,
a tether to lure me home.

Today you force the issue —
some archaic baptism.
Pushing out with violence,
you cause me to slide.

Underneath I hear a chugging —
limbs in a seaweed salad
of contorted faces,
cries of help,
muffling
at the threshold —
Medusa's raft.

I sink,
sensing the pulse of the moon,
belly emptied of human need,
the landscape primed for gestation.
I emerge as a blastocyst.
Afloat, in liquid space
between my eye
and your fist.

Suture Clamp

Zinnia fire.

Skies explode.
Smiles break through an overcast mood —
a chair so large,
a kiss too hard.

Attempt to home in the roving,
the promised cue.
I place a mark,
identify the part.

A sign,
a sneer,
a wig to conceal
my IQ.

Its peaks and deficits
colossal,
the sun scored out,
my hat gigantic.
I have to
duck to pass
through doors.

Born to It

I want you, I need you
but I don't know how
to love you.

When you ignore me
I can't bear it.
You seem to know
how to love yourself
but deny me
that simple grace.

I take that back.
You only want
everything I can give,
which is a lot,
but never enough.

If I could love you
without running out ...
wouldn't that be grand?
Can we work at it together?

Is this a fair exchange?
A trading of vulnerabilities.
Tell me if I'm asking
too much.

Like giving birth,
love comes into being.
Essentially learned,
we are born into it,
like gravity.

Man-Oil

Was it the egg that broke first
or the child who severed the hand
from the wrist, head from the neck,
leg from the hip?

Hard to know with the popping sound
in the ear. One thing is for sure —
the arrow shot through,
internal space has expanded.

Up close the wave pattern is erratic,
wrestling on a stack of pillows.
A peculiar smell of man-oil
permeates the chamber.

Stars, planets, and people collide —
their familiar patterns woven in silk,
cushions festooned with bells and tassels,
scenes of battle.

Nation-states are plundered
and a surge of volunteers
line up to provide support.
Is it safe to undress?

Be Careful with Hope

It takes off and shoots an arrow
at impossible targets,
tumbles down at the child's feet
after a gasp of terror.
Hope returns
and recalls an expensive item,
shiny and luminous,
a trinket that eventually ends up
in a rummage sale bin.

In too many ways
hope comes up
when relationships
are crashing down.
Despite intermittent resistance
and stabs at self-protection,
hope hovers without a home.
It comes through as inspired banter,
firm handshakes, shoulder patting.

Hope is silent in the rhythm of conversation,
like weather, mutable and transient.
Without it one may give up altogether.

Initially raw and shapeless,
disguised as a remedy for suffering,
rampant hope requires apprehension.

The trick is to warm it in the hands,
sculpt it into something
worth keeping.

IVF

The gate to the playpen is open,
the chicks are roaming free,
away from the pillow of home.

Some have learned to fly by jumping —
and for a moment they suspend in the air.
Held in the arms of uplift, of will over gravity.

Icarus was a scientist who believed in the magic of flight.
He calculated the distance up,
though lost his notes on the way back down.

The horse drawn chariot took him higher into the clouds,
a projectile of spit to sperm.
Ariel remembers Icarus as she hovers over his grave.

Casting a shade on the page of descent,
she claims the fugue of his button-downed moan,
a sputter adrift inscrutable space.

She holds a bent straw,
extracts a few ovaries.
Siphons them into a petri dish.

Perforates the ovum with a needle and slides it in.
Embryos begin to flourish,
replicating crystals, webs and skin.

The best planted in her womb.
Nine months later, the land is broken,
and the rivers push out to the sea.

Aesop's Tale of the Two Pots

How to preserve a gallon of water
in a drought.

The colonizers carry metal pails
while the locals hold clay pots.

The collective body is thrust out
as a defense
against loss.

A container for the heart beat
that defies oppression
by simply being with

complexity,
the strain.

Meandering across the landscape
while the biped creates a database,

a dimensional enclosure
containing a voice

within and for itself.

Archimedes Screw

Good work old fella, inventing the spiral,
honouring the twisted placenta, the pig's penis,

and caring for the bulb,
the fruit on the stem, but also

knowing that when the fruit is ripe
it will break free.

What are the terms of this contractual agreement?
How can one be safe when the auger is turning?

In suffering thou shalt bring forth children—
the biblical case for natural birth.

Being born is the first challenge,
leaving the earth is harder still.

So get ready,
it doesn't get any easier

to determine what is yours
and what is mine.

Early Morning

The child man in a trench coat
looked through me today
as though I was the breast
that cared for him once.

His eyes were wide
and his mouth agape.
The moment enlarged
to contain us,
then narrowed inward.
His whiskers framed a cloud
that rose with the dust
above our heads.

I recognized him
from some familiar place.
We had done this before,
a kind of mutual gazing
apprehending
and blinking in.

The subway doors closed
and he was absorbed
by the crowd.
I may see him again
possibly not,
more likely tomorrow.

We won't speak.
We will simply listen
in
and wait.

On Offer

A tyrant,
a charismatic leader,
an oppressor who required others to follow.

An act of ritual conscription,
the aspirant giving way.
Naturally a revolution ensued,
a relativistic problem.

Must the tyrant be disarmed,
or internalized?
No, neither.
Knead at the edge of panic,
known.

Displaced,
divided and shaped
until it becomes one's own.

Doing It with Intention

Planning to greet you with respect —
Good morning.

Smile,
mutual hmmmm.

An invitation to be in the glimmer,
present in the crawlspace of sleep,

the bleary self
drawn out,

held down,
fed

line-by-line
a nourishing meal

of past, present, future
all at once.

Time drills down
in the nomenclature room.

Playing with Your Pet

I am part animal, part human.
The human in me can lie down
and behave, accept repose.
The territories drawn.

Even though the animal in me
wants to knock you down,
I have learned to respect the line
of touch me here, but not there.

I fly above the safe zone,
encounter a surge of longing.
Sliding through the sweaty convulsion,
putting up with the foggy lens.

I emerge alone and sated,
losing my dignity and gaining a secret.
Ignited by a mutual gaze,
an alignment from within.

Intrepid at the brink of the belly.
I eat you whole.

Crossing Over

A boundary
demarcated by screens and ropes
between the sacred and the profane.

I want to touch the relics
the power,
the potentiality:

Non toccare grazie.

Broken parts swept away,
made solo,
catalogued
and placed behind glass.

Lost and Found signs
are posted everywhere.
It is better to be alone
than lost

in
someone else.

Conduct Oneself in the Presence

Of others.
Be a witness.

Appear cooperative,
Orderly. Attend to the revolution

Within.
Social controls are just that.

Leave them at the door,
like shoes.

Paradox

The splendid annihilation of belonging
to a puzzle,
suspended in the moment
of speculation.

Not wanting anything
from the other,
just a deviation.
Pretending to want nothing—

so neglect can be
avoided,
again.

Company of One

The "I" is important,
the inverse of how it was.

Displacement of past wrongs,
the emancipation project.

Armed and able,
I take my piece of the pie,

eat the filling
and leave the crust.

The remedy is unacceptable
unless the "I" is recognized.

Being seen and counted,
"I" am only this once.

Allegory of the Journey

Go outside,
be guided,
be told where to go.

Wait behind the curtain,
touch the velvet presence,
maintain, control.

Passion in space is ambidextrous,
so go and wander,
show us what is and what is not.

Listen,
hear it again.
Differently.

Acknowledgements

Thank you to the editors of these journals for publishing the following poems, some of which have been modified:

Canthius: "Finding Without Looking"
Lacewing: "Lake Huggers"
The Ekphrastic Review: "Self-Portrait"
The Fiddlehead: "Farewell to Woodsyman"

Special thanks are owed to Elana Wolff for her editorial insights, to publishers Connie McParland and Michael Mirolla, and the staff at Guernica Editions for their dedication and support.

About the Author

Carol Barbour is a graduate of the Ontario College of Art and the University of Toronto (MA, Art History). She has exhibited paintings, sculptures and artist books at galleries and book fairs in Canada, the United States, and Europe. Her poems, essays, and fiction are published by literary and arts journals including *Sein und Werden, Transverse, Matriart, Resources for Feminist Research, The Toronto Quarterly,* and *Impulse.* Her hand-made artist books, which combine art and writing, are collected by the National Gallery of Canada, Artexte, the British Library, Goldsmiths, University of London, the Museum of Modern Art, the Banff Art Centre, and others. She has presented her research on early modern art and books at the Renaissance Society of America, Biblyon, and the International Society of Emblems conference.

Printed in July 2018
by Gauvin Press,
Gatineau, Québec